# CHRISTIAN SCIENCE HYMNAL

## SUPPLEMENT

### HYMNS 430–462

Marca Registrada

The Christian Science Publishing Society
Boston, Massachusetts, USA

The Church Dome and Tower Medallion
is a registered trademark of The Christian Science Board of Directors.
Used by permission.

ISBN 978-0-87510-468-3

Printed in the USA.

# PREFACE

Welcome to the 2008 *Christian Science Hymnal Supplement.* We invite you to join with Christian Scientists around the world who are using this new collection of hymns in church services and as inspiration for their healing work. The hymns in this *Supplement* are the first additions to the *Christian Science Hymnal* since 1932 and are presented as an extension to the *Hymnal* and not a replacement. It may be interesting to note that the first *Christian Science Hymnal Supplement* was released simultaneously with the current *Christian Science Hymnal* in 1932. It consists of 29 hymns (numbers 401–429) and has always been bound into the back of the *Hymnal.* This new *Supplement*, published as a separate volume, contains 33 hymns (430–462) arranged in alphabetical order by the first line of their text and numbered to follow the previous *Supplement* in the *Hymnal.* This number methodology is the same used in the 1932 edition of the *Christian Science Hymnal.*

## SELECTION OF THE *SUPPLEMENT* HYMNS

This collection expands our musical palette. Some of the hymns were written specifically for this *Supplement*, while some are common to other Christian hymnals. A number of the hymns are familiar texts set to new tunes. Several tunes reflect or blend musical styles that have not previously been included in our *Hymnal*: folk, country, pop, jazz, as well as African and Caribbean themes are included. Some of these new styles make use of syncopated rhythms, the "blue" notes of the scale, and contemporary harmonic progressions. In some cases spiritual songs, restructured as hymns, expand beyond the traditional hymn form.

## NOTATION

Though the notation standards established in the 1932 edition of the *Christian Science Hymnal* are followed, there are a few new methods of notation employed in this *Supplement.*

At the beginning of each hymn a metronome marking is given. (In the *Hymnal,* these are listed in an Index.) Observing this marking is essential to interpreting the hymn correctly.

Several hymns include chord symbols, which gives the accompanist the freedom to improvise.

Those hymns written in a "popular song" style, in verse/chorus form, are longer than traditional hymns and require 3 or 4 pages to notate. Several others also require more than two pages of notation, which necessitates turning pages while singing these hymns.

Many hymns have repeat signs for certain sections which are important for the accompanist and singers to observe. A few necessitate turning pages back to repeat the entire section.

The numbers following the name of the hymn tune (at the top left of the music) indicate the poetic meter of the text, that is, the number of syllables in each line of text. It should be acknowledged that several of the hymns have such irregular texts that no poetic meter could be assigned.

When the poetic meter changes from one verse to the next within a hymn, the musical notation accommodates this change with the use of small note heads. This is the same as the notation used in the 1932 *Christian Science Hymnal*.

Great effort has been made to make these hymns accessible to a wide range of musical abilities. Selections are written in a comfortable vocal range for most people and in simpler keys for instrumental accompaniment. In some cases only the accompaniment part and unison vocal line are included, instead of the traditional four-part vocal format.

## Hymn Texts

There are new alternative settings to five of Mrs. Eddy's poems: "Christmas Morn" (two versions), "Love" (two versions), "Satisfied," the "Communion Hymn," and "'Feed My Sheep.'" There are also new settings of six other texts from the *Hymnal*. All of these are listed in the Index. The other 20 hymn texts include poems previously published in the *Christian Science Sentinel* or *The Christian Science Journal*, hymns borrowed from other hymnals, as well as some original works which are published here for the first time.

## Indexes

"Indexes" are also provided for the tune names, poetic meter, composers, and authors, and may be used in conjunction with the "Indexes" in the *Hymnal*.

## Acknowledgements

Much appreciation is due those who submitted selections for this publication and to those who granted permission for use of their copyrighted material. Where copyright permission is not shown, rights are held by the Christian Science Board of Directors or The Christian Science Publishing Society, or are in the public domain. Inquiries regarding copyright and requests for permission to use hymns from the *Supplement* should be directed to the Publishing Society or directly to the copyright owners when their permission is noted with the hymn.

Over many years tremendous thought and supportive prayers have been devoted to the development of new music for the *Christian Science Hymnal*. To all those who have contributed to this activity directly and indirectly we offer our deepest gratitude.

The Christian Science Publishing Society

# 430

**MICHAEL** 8.7.8.7.3.3.7.
**HERBERT HOWELLS**

**JOACHIM NEANDER**
Adapted by **ROBERT BRIDGES**
Adapted by **FENELLA BENNETTS**

1. All my hope on God is found - ed; Day by day my
2. Earth - ly treas-ures, pride and glo - ry, Hu - man power and
3. Dai - ly does th'al might - y Giv - er Boun - teous gifts on
4. Now from man to God e - ter - nal End - less thanks and

trust is new. Through the trials of life He guides me,
world - ly trust, Though with care and toil are build - ed,
us be - stow. His de - sire our soul de - light - eth,
praise be sung. Hearts made new are an - thems rais - ing

Music by Herbert Howells
Words by Joachim Neander (d.1680) adpt. by Robert Bridges (d.1930)
© Copyright 1968 Novello & Company Limited.
All Rights Reserved. International Copyright Secured.
Used by Permission.
Words adpt. © 2008 Fenella Bennetts.

# 431

**NEW BRITAIN** C.M.
Traditional American melody
Arranged by **ROBERT ROCKABRAND**

**JOHN NEWTON**
Adapted

1. A - maz - ing grace! how sweet the sound, That saved a
2. 'Twas grace that taught my heart to fear, And grace my
3. Through man - y dan - gers, toils, and snares, I have al -
4. The Lord has prom - ised good to me, His word my

soul like me. I once was lost, but
fears re - lieved; How pre - cious did that
read - y come; 'Tis grace has brought me
hope se - cures; He will my shield and

now am found, Was blind, but now I see.
grace ap - pear The hour I first be - lieved!
safe thus far, And grace will lead me home.
por - tion be As long as life en - dures.

# 432

**NEWBORN** 8.4.8.4.
**FENELLA BENNETTS**

CHRISTMAS MORN
**MARY BAKER EDDY**

1. Blest Christ - mas morn, though murk - y clouds Pur - sue thy way, Thy light was born where storm en-shrouds Nor dawn nor day!

2. Dear Christ, for-ev - er

*These words have other settings. See Hymn Nos. 23–28 and 433.*

# 433

**HODGSON** 8.4.8.4.
**ROBERT ROCKABRAND**

CHRISTMAS MORN
**MARY BAKER EDDY**

1. Blest Christ-mas morn, though murk-y clouds Pur-sue thy way, Thy light was born where storm en-shrouds Nor dawn nor day!

3. Thou God-i-de-a, Life-en-crowned, The Beth-lehem babe— Be-loved, re-plete, by flesh em-bound—Was but thy shade!

5. Or cru-el creed, or earth-born taint: Fill us to-day With all thou art— be thou our saint, Our stay, al-way.

2. Dear Christ, for-ev-er here and near, No cra-dle song, No na-tal hour and moth-er's tear, To thee be-long.

4. Thou gen-tle beam of liv-ing Love, And death-less Life! Truth in-fi-nite,— so far a-bove All mor-tal strife,

Music © 2008 The Christian Science Board of Directors.

*These words have other settings. See Hymn Nos. 23–28 and 432.*

# 434

NOCTURNE 86.86.88.
PETER B. ALLEN

LOVE
MARY BAKER EDDY

♩ = 62   Mixed Meter

1. Brood o'er us with Thy shel-t'ring wing, 'Neath which our
4. Through God, who gave that word of might Which swelled cre -

spir - its blend Like broth-er birds, that soar and sing,
a - tion's lay: "Let there be light, and there was light."

And on the same branch bend. The ar - row that doth
What chased the clouds a - way? 'Twas Love whose fin - ger

wound the dove Darts not from those who watch and
traced a - loud A bow of prom - ise on the

Music © 2008 The Christian Science Board of Directors.

*These words have other settings. See Hymn Nos. 30–32 and 435.*

love.
cloud.

2. If thou the bend - ing reed wouldst break  By
3. Learn, too, that wis - dom's rod is given  For
5. Thou to whose power our hope we give,  Free

thought or word un - kind,
faith to kiss, and know;
us from hu - man strife.

Pray that his spir - it you par -
That greet-ings glo - rious from high
Fed by Thy love di - vine we

*Last time to Coda*

take,
heaven,
live,

Who loved and healed man - kind:
Whence joys su - per - nal flow,
For Love a - lone is Life;

Seek
Come
And

ho - ly thoughts and heaven - ly strain,
from that Love, di - vine - ly near,

(2.) That make men one in love re - main.

(3.) Which chast - ens pride and earth - born fear,

*D. C. al Coda*

*Coda*

(5.) life most sweet, as heart to heart Speaks kind - ly when we meet and part.

# 435

**BROTHER JAMES' AIR** 86.86.88.
**JAMES LEITH MACBETH BAIN**
Adapted by **ROBERT ROCKABRAND**

LOVE
**MARY BAKER EDDY**

1. Brood o'er us with Thy shel - t'ring wing, 'Neath which our spir - its
2. If thou the bend - ing reed wouldst break By thought or word un -
3. Learn, too, that wis-dom's rod is given For faith to kiss, and
4. Through God, who gave that word of might Which swelled cre - a - tion's
5. Thou to whose power our hope we give, Free us from hu - man

blend Like broth - er birds, that soar and sing, And
kind, Pray that his spir - it you par - take, Who
know; That greet-ings glo - rious from high heaven, Whence
lay: "Let there be light, and there was light." What
strife. Fed by Thy love di - vine we live, For

on the same branch bend. The ar - row that doth
loved and healed man - kind: Seek ho - ly thoughts and
joys su - per - nal flow, Come from that Love, di -
chased the clouds a - way? 'Twas Love whose fin - ger
Love a - lone is Life; And life most sweet, as

*These words have other settings. See Hymn Nos. 30–32 and 434.*

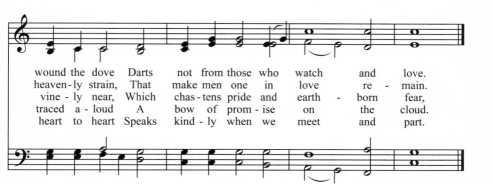

wound the dove Darts   not from those who   watch   and   love.
heaven-ly strain, That   make men one  in   love   re - main.
vine - ly near, Which   chas-tens pride and   earth - born   fear,
traced a - loud   A   bow of prom - ise   on   the   cloud.
heart to heart Speaks   kind - ly when we   meet   and   part.

# 436

ORCHARDS L.M.
ANDREW D. BREWIS

SIMON BROWNE
Adapted

1. Come, gra-cious Spir-it, heaven-ly Love,
2. The light of Truth to us dis-play,

With light and com-fort from a-bove;
That we may know and choose Thy way;

Be Thou our guard-ian, Thou our guide, O'er
Plant ho-ly joy in ev-ery heart, That

*These words have another setting. See Hymn No. 39.*

Way, Nor let us from thy pre - cepts

stray; Lead us to God, our heaven - ly

rest, That we may be for - ev - er

blest, For - ev - er blest.

# 437

UNION SEMINARY 88.7.88.9.
HAROLD FRIEDELL
Arranged by JET TURNER

COMMUNION
VIOLET HAY

1. Fa - ther, Thou art ver - y near us, Well we
2. Christ, the way of our sal - va - tion, Rends the
3. Fa - ther, this most won - drous un - ion We would

know that Thou dost hear us, And dost
veil of sep - a - ra - tion, Shews our
prove in blest com - mun - ion: Take Thy

an - swer ere we call: May the prayer of
life in Spir - it, free— Shews the glo - ry
Truth, our bread from heav - en, Drink the wine of

faith now heal us,    May the vi - sion true re -
of cre - a - tion,    God and man in true re -
in - spi - ra - tion,    Rise in ho - ly ex - al -

veal us One with Thee, and Thou our all in all.
la - tion: Now, be - lov - ed, sons of God are we!
ta - tion, One in Thee, re - deemed, re - stored, for - given.

# 438

8.7.8.7.D.

**JOY TESSMAN and SCOTT MARTIN**
Arranged

**ELIZABETH C. ADAMS**

1. Fa - ther, we Thy lov - ing chil - dren Lift our hearts in joy to - day,
2. Come we dai - ly then, dear Fa - ther, O - pen hearts and will - ing hands,
3. In Thy house se - cure - ly dwell-ing, Where Thy chil - dren live to bless,
4. Fa - ther, we Thy lov - ing chil-dren Lift our hearts in joy to - day,

Know-ing well that Thou wilt keep us Ev - er in Thy bless - ed way.
Ea - ger ears, ex - pect-ant, joy-ful, Read-y for Thy right com - mands.
See - ing on - ly Thy cre - a - tion, We can share Thy hap - pi - ness,
Know-ing well that Thou wilt keep us Ev - er in Thy bless - ed way.

Thou art Love and Thou art wis - dom, Thou art Life and Thou art All;
We would hear no oth - er voic - es, We would heed no oth - er call;
Share Thy joy and spend it free - ly. Loy - al hearts can feel no fear;

In Thy Spir - it liv - ing, mov - ing, We shall nei - ther faint nor fall.
Thou a - lone art good and gra-cious, Thou our Mind and Thou our All.
We Thy chil-dren know Thee, Fa - ther, Love and Life for - ev - er near.

*These words have another setting. See Hymn No. 58.*

# 439

Natalie Sleeth
Adapted from Scripture

6.7.6.6.7.5.7.5.
Natalie Sleeth

♩ = 42-46    *Unison*

Feed my lambs, tend my sheep, O - ver all a vig - il keep;

In my name lead them forth gen - tly as a shep - herd.

1. When they wan - der, when they stray, their pro - tec - tor be.
2. Un - to all who lose the way, hope and com - fort be.

As ye do un - to my flock, thus ye do to me.
As ye do un - to my flock, thus ye do to me.

Feed my lambs, tend my sheep, O - ver all a vig - il keep;

In my name lead them forth gen - tly, gen - tly

as a lov - ing shep-herd of the Lord.

# 440

ABBOT'S LEIGH 8.7.8.7.D.
CYRIL V. TAYLOR

JOHN NEWTON
Adapted

♩ = 96-100

1. Glo - rious things of thee are spo - ken, Zi - on,
2. Round each hab - i - ta - tion hov-ering, See the
3. See, the streams of liv - ing wa - ters, Spring - ing

cit - y of our God; He whose word can - not be
cloud and fire ap - pear For a glo - ry and a
from e - ter - nal Love, Well sup - ply thy sons and

bro - ken, Formed thee for His own a - bode:
cov - ering, Show - ing that the Lord is near.
daugh - ters, And all fear of want re - move.

On the Rock of A - ges found - ed, What can shake thy
Thus de - riv - ing from their ban - ner, Light by night, and
Who can faint, while such a riv - er Ev - er shall their

*These words have another setting. See Hymn No. 71.*

sure    re - pose?    By    sal - va - tion's    walls    sur -
shade    by    day,    Safe    they    feed    up - on    the
thirst    as - suage,—    Grace,    which    like    the    Lord,    the

round - ed    Thou    mayst    smile    at    all    thy    foes.
man - na,    Which    He    gives    them    when    they    pray.
giv - er,    Nev - er    fails    from    age    to    age?

# 441

Traditional Caribbean song
and **HAL H. HOPSON**
Arranged by **HAL H. HOPSON**

Traditional Caribbean and
additional text based on
Psalm 150 by **HAL H. HOPSON**

* Optional four-bar introduction.

*Verse*

1. Praise God in this ho - ly place, ev - ery na - tion, ev - ery race.
2. Ev - ery-thing that breathes now praise, sing your songs, let voic - es raise.

Come, make joy - ful mu - sic to the Lord.
Come, make joy - ful mu - sic to the Lord.

Sound the trum - pet, sound it clear, sound it for the world to hear.
Play the cym - bals, play the lute; play the tim - brel, play the flute.

Come, make joy - ful mus - ic to the Lord.
Come, make joy - ful mus - ic to the Lord.

*for final refrain*

# 442

**SANTA ROSA** 8.7.8.7.D.
**PETER B. ALLEN**

**MARIA LOUISE BAUM**

1. Here, O God, Thy heal-ing pres-ence Lifts our thoughts from self and sin,
2. Rev-erent lives un-veil Thy beau-ty, Faith-ful wit-ness bear of Thee;

Fills with light their hid-den plac-es, When Thy love is wel-comed in. Here Thy ten-der
Bind-ing up the bro-ken-heart-ed, We re-flect Thy ra-dian-cy. So may deep-er

sweet per-sua-sions Turn us home to heaven-ly ways, While our hearts, un-
con-se-cra-tion Show Thee forth in heal-ing's sign, Till through joy - ful

**1.** **2.**

sealed, a-dor-ing, Pour the fra-grance of Thy praise.
self-sur-ren-der We in Love's pure like-ness shine.

*These words have other settings. See Hymn Nos. 109 and 110.*

# 443

**O WALY, WALY** L.M.
Scottish folk song
Arranged by **ROBERT ROCKABRAND**

HOME
**ROSEMARY COBHAM**

1. Home is the con - scious-ness of good That holds us
2. Our Fa - ther's house has man - y rooms, And each with
3. Home is the Fa - ther's sweet "Well done," God's dai - ly,

in its wide em - brace; The stead - y light that com - forts
peace and love im - bued; No child can ev - er stray be -
hour - ly gift of grace. We go to meet our broth - er's

us In ev - ery path our foot - steps trace.
yond The com - pass of in - fin - i - tude.
need, And find our home in ev - ery place.

# 444

**I AM THE LORD**
DÉSIRÉE GOYETTE

**DÉSIRÉE GOYETTE**
based on Isaiah 45:5–6

1. I am the Lord, there is none else; There is no God be-
2. I am the Truth, there is none else; There is no Truth be-
3. In - no - cent one, sin - less and pure, Noth-ing can ev - er di-

side Me. I gird - ed thee, I gird - ed thee,
side Me. In - fi - nite light, boun - ti - ful, bright,
vide thee. Gov - erned by Love, you're safe and se - cure;

Though thou hast not e - ven known Me. But know that from the
Is ev - er pres - ent to guide thee. Be - loved and free, e -
I am for - ev - er be - side thee. So rest and know wher-

ris - ing sun To the west there is none be - side Me, For
ter - nal - ly, Per - fect peace and joy I pro - vide thee, For
e're you go, Home and heav'n can - not be de - nied thee, For

I am the Lord, there is none else; There is no God be - side Me.

# 445

**DALTON**
SUSAN MACK

SUSAN MACK

1. I a - wake each morn to a brand - new day, Sing - ing
2. (I can) walk with Love through the val - ley of fear, Sing - ing

Hal - le - lu - jah! as I go on my way, For my heart is
Hal - le - lu - jah! my Sav - ior is here! The des - ert of my

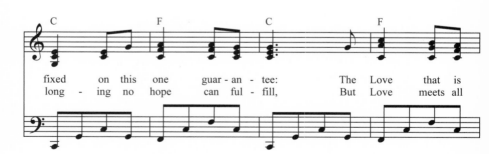

fixed on this one guar - an - tee: The Love that is
long - ing no hope can ful - fill, But Love meets all

mat - ter the need and no mat - ter the threat, I'm se -

cure in Your love, no fear, no re - gret. Can there

be a sweet - er com - fort, a grace more di - vine, Than the

thought that Your love is here and is mine? Ten - der

# 446

**HERNANDEZ**
**FRANK HERNANDEZ**

**FRANK HERNANDEZ**
Based on Psalm 145

I will bless the Lord and give Him glo - ry. O I will bless His name and give Him glo - ry. The Lord is gra - cious and mer - ci - ful,

"I Will Bless the Lord."
© 1981 by Candle Company Music.

ry.    O    I         will         bless    His    name    and

1. Optional Repeat                    *D. C.*

give    Him         glo    -    ry.

2. Final Ending

*rit.*

ry,    and    give         Him         glo    -    ry.

# 447

**MKHAYA** 8.4.8.4.
**ANDREW D. BREWIS**

SATISFIED
**MARY BAKER EDDY**

1. It mat - ters not what be thy lot, So Love doth
3. Aye, dark - ling sense, a - rise, go hence! Our God is

guide; For storm or shine, pure peace is thine, What-
good. False fears are foes— truth tat - ters those, When

e'er be - tide. 2. And of these stones, or
un - der - stood. 4. Love loos - eth thee, and

Music © 2008 The Christian Science Board of Directors.

*These words have other settings. See Hymn Nos. 160–162.*

# 448

**LASST UNS ERFREUEN** 8.8.4.4.D.
Geistliche Kirchengesang, 1623; alt.
Harmonized by **R. Vaughan Williams**

LO! THEY THAT FOLLOW
AFTER GOOD
**Violet Hay**

1. Lo! they that fol-low af-ter good, By them God's word is un-der-
2. O ye to whom God's word is known, Make you His prom-is-es your

stood, So they prove Him, Praise and prove Him! Through them He doth per-form His
own, Rise and prove Him, Praise and prove Him! His might-y love and ho-ly

will, To them His prom-is-es ful-fil, For they love Him! Laud and
power Are here to bless us ev-ery hour, Let us love Him! Laud and

love Him! Al-le-lu-ia, Al-le-lu-ia, Al-le-lu-ia!
love Him! Al-le-lu-ia, Al-le-lu-ia, Al-le-lu-ia!

Music LASST UNS ERFREUEN arr. Ralph Vaughan Williams (1872-1958)
from The English Hymnal by permission of Oxford University Press.

# 449

**ENDLESS SONG** 8.7.8.7.D.
**ROBERT LOWRY**
Arranged by **ROBERT ROCKABRAND**

ROBERT LOWRY

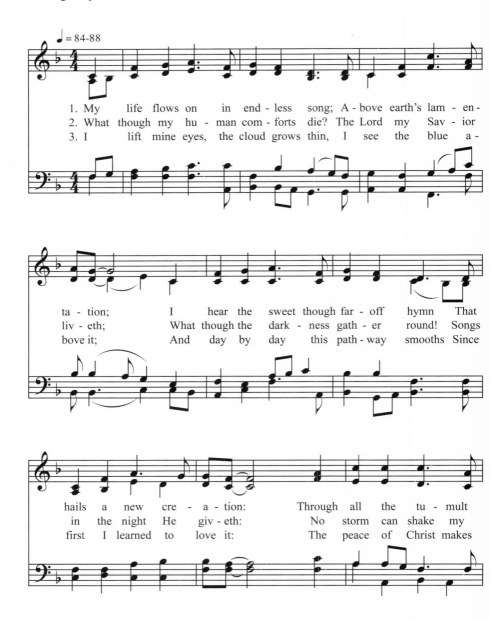

♩ = 84-88

1. My life flows on in end - less song; A - bove earth's lam - en -
2. What though my hu - man com - forts die? The Lord my Sav - ior
3. I lift mine eyes, the cloud grows thin, I see the blue a -

ta - tion; I hear the sweet though far - off hymn That
liv - eth; What though the dark - ness gath - er round! Songs
bove it; And day by day this path - way smooths Since

hails a new cre - a - tion: Through all the tu - mult
in the night He giv - eth: No storm can shake my
first I learned to love it: The peace of Christ makes

and the strife    I hear the    mu - sic ring - ing,    It
in - most calm    While to    that    Rock    I'm cling - ing,    Since
fresh my heart,    A foun - tain    ev - er spring - ing,    All

finds an ech - o    in    my soul, How can I    keep    from sing - ing?
Love is Lord of    heav'n and earth, How can I    keep    from sing - ing?
things are mine since I    am His, How can I    keep    from sing - ing?

# 450

MORA PROCTOR 11.10.11.10.
WILLIAM J. REYNOLDS

RUBY NILSON

1. O house of God, built on a firm foun - da - tion,
2. We hear the Word, in song and ser - mon spo - ken,
3. O Fa - ther, feed us with Thy bread from heav - en,
4. We feel Thy peace, Thine arms of Love en - fold - ing,

Stand - ing se - cure a - mid the storms of life,
In si - lent prayer, we turn to God to - day;
The liv - ing wa - ter, may we drink of Thee,
We lift our hearts in praise and grat - i - tude,

Where all may come to learn of true sal - va - tion
Our hum - ble hearts re - ceive the bless - ed to - ken
And ev - ery les - son which Thy love hath giv - en
And from this hour, a glimpse of heaven be - hold - ing,

And find re - lease from dis - cord, pain, and strife.
Of Truth that guides us in the up - ward way.
Oh, may we learn it with hu - mil - i - ty.
Go forth at last, our joy and strength re - newed.

# 451

**SHERWOOD** L.M.
**PETER B. ALLEN**

**JOHN GREENLEAF WHITTIER**
Adapted

♪ = 126-138

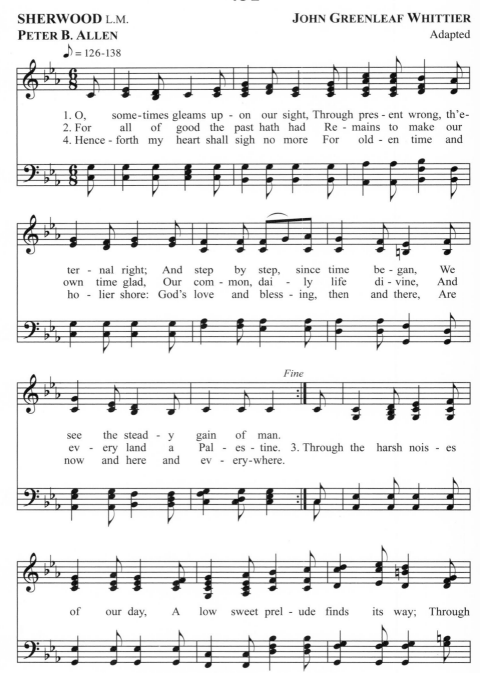

1. O,        some-times gleams up - on  our sight, Through pres - ent  wrong, th'e-
2. For     all   of   good  the  past  hath  had    Re - mains  to   make   our
4. Hence - forth  my   heart  shall  sigh  no  more   For    old - en   time   and

ter - nal right;  And  step    by  step,  since  time   be - gan,   We
own  time  glad,  Our  com - mon, dai - ly  life   di - vine,  And
ho - lier  shore: God's  love  and  bless - ing,  then  and  there,  Are

*Fine*

see   the  stead - y   gain   of  man.
ev - ery  land    a    Pal - es - tine.  3. Through  the   harsh  nois - es
now   and  here   and   ev - ery-where.

of     our  day,  A   low  sweet  prel - ude  finds  its  way;  Through

Music © 2008 Peter B. Allen. Used by permission.

*These words have other settings. See Hymn Nos. 238 and 239.*

clouds of doubt and creeds of fear    A light is break-ing, calm and clear.

# 452

NEWFOUND Irregular
SUSAN MACK
Arranged by SUE and CAREY LOOMIS

O THOU UNCHANGING TRUTH
PETER J. HENNIKER-HEATON

1. O Thou un-chang-ing Truth, whose facts e-ter-nal give
2. O Thou a-bun-dant Life, whose fresh-ness dai-ly ad-
3. O Thou, O bound-less Love, for-ev-er un-di-min-ished,

us the cour-age to out-face the storm, to
mits no com-mon round, no dull rou-tine, this
how far and lit-tle seems the lie of pain. We

rise a-gainst the sens-es' swift a-larm and
is our joy and this our dis-ci-pline, to
were with Thee, be-fore the world be-gan, and

stand un-moved at Spir-it's high tri-bu-nal, Thy
take Thy gift of life and use it ful-ly; this
shall be with Thee, when the world has van-ished; Thy

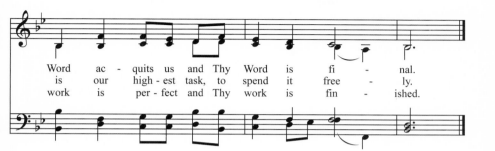

Word    ac - quits us  and  Thy  Word  is   fi   -   nal.
is     our   high - est  task,  to  spend  it   free   -   ly.
work    is   per - fect  and  Thy  work  is   fin   -   ished.

# 453

**RISE UP**
PETER B. ALLEN

PETER B. ALLEN

♩. = 60-62, Boldly

1. Rise up and walk, take up your bed. With these few words the
2. Cleanse the lep - ers, heal the sick. Cast out de - mons.

sick - ness fled. Stretch forth your hand. Re - ceive your sight.
Raise the dead. Truth is re - vealed in ev - ery place,

Je - sus' com-mands re - veal God's might. You are God's pur - pose,
Through-out all time, through-out all space. Right in this mo - ment,

His great de - sign. Beau - ti - ful, blame-less, His child di - vine.
do - ing God's will "These works shall you do, and great - er still."

Hold-ing your thought to the good and the true, Spir-it will form you a-
Stand-ing tri-um-phant up-on ho-ly ground, Songs of the an-gels re-

*Refrain*

new.
sound. Rise up and walk! God made you free,

born of His lib - er - ty. Care-free and strong,

you are His song, per - fect for all to see.

Moun-tains and seas, great ris - ing trees, e - cho the joy - ous

song: Heav-en is here, har - mo-ny's bliss

to ev-ery-one be - longs.

# 454

DÉSIRÉE GOYETTE 10.7.7.7.9.

COMMUNION HYMN
**MARY BAKER EDDY**

♩ = 58, Tenderly

*Unison*

1. Saw ye my Sav - iour? Heard ye the glad sound?
2. Mourn - er, it calls you,— "Come to my bos - om,

Felt ye the pow-er of the Word? 'Twas the
Love wipes your tears all a - way, And will

Truth that made us free, And was found by you and
lift the shade of gloom, And for you make ra - diant

Music © 2008 The Christian Science Board of Directors.

*These words have other settings. See Hymn Nos. 298–302.*

me In the life and the love of our Lord.
room Midst the glo - ries of one end-less

day."

3. Sin - ner, it calls you,—

"Come to this foun - tain, Cleanse the foul sens - es with -

in; 'Tis the Spir-it that makes pure, That ex -

alts thee, and will cure All thy sor - row and sick - ness and

sin." 4. Strong - est de - liv - er - er,

friend of the friend - less, Life of all be - ing di -

# 455

**LAFFERTY**
**KAREN LAFFERTY**

KAREN LAFFERTY

# 456

**HOW TO SOW** 7.5.7.5.D.
**ROBERT ROCKABRAND**

**"FEED MY SHEEP"**
**MARY BAKER EDDY**

♩ = 104-108

1. Shep - herd, show me how to go  O'er the hill - side steep,
2. Thou wilt bind the stub - born will,  Wound the cal - lous breast,
3. So, when day grows dark and cold,  Tear or tri - umph harms,

How to gath - er, how to sow,—  How to feed Thy sheep;
Make self - right - eous - ness be still,  Break earth's stu - pid rest.
Lead Thy lamb - kins to the fold,  Take them in Thine arms;

I will lis - ten for Thy voice,  Lest my foot - steps stray;
Stran - gers on a bar - ren shore,  La - b'ring long and lone,
Feed the hun - gry, heal the heart,  Till the morn - ing's beam;

I will fol - low and re - joice  All the rug - ged way.
We would en - ter by the door,  And Thou know'st Thine own;
White as wool, ere they de - part,  Shep - herd, wash them clean.

*These words have other settings. See Hymn Nos. 304–309.*

# 457

CONSECRATION 77.77.77.
FENELLA BENNETTS

FRANCES R. HAVERGAL
Adapted

1. Take my life, and let it be Con - se - crat - ed, Lord, to Thee.
2. Take my feet, and let them be Swift and beau - ti - ful for Thee.

Take my mo - ments and my days, Let them flow in cease - less praise.
Take my voice, and let me sing Al - ways, on - ly, for my King.

Take my hands, and let them move At the im - pulse of Thy love.
Take my lips, and let them be Filled with mes - sa - ges from Thee.

*These words have another setting. See Hymn No. 324.*

# 458

**O WALY, WALY** L.M.
Scottish folk song
Arranged by **FENELLA BENNETTS**

THE VOICE OF LOVE
**FENELLA BENNETTS**
Based on I Corinthians 13

♩ = 62-64

1. Though I may speak with mov-ing words, Which can in-
2. Though I may give my world-ly goods With-out a
3. Though I may search the deep-est books, Com-pan-ion
4. Now I would learn to know this Love Through meek and

spire the heart of man, But have no love — to seal their
thought of self or gain, Un-less they bear the fruits of
with the wis-est men, God's lov-ing voice still calls to
pa - tient min-is - try, Un-til my life has grown a-

worth, They are but emp - ti-ness and sham.
love They are as clouds with-out their rain.
me, It bids me turn and look a - gain.
new And Love is All - in - all to me.

# 459

KEDDY C.M.
EDWIN R. TAYLOR

RUTH C. DUCK

♩ = 120-126 *Unison*

1. To God com - pose a song of joy; To God make
2. Be - fore the na - tions God re - veals A just and
3. In ev - ery cor - ner of the earth, God comes to
4. With trum - pet, with the sound of horns, With strings, yes,
5. Let seas in all their full - ness roar, And peo - ple
6. The God of jus - tice comes to save; Let earth make

mel - o - dy, Whose arm of strength does won - drous
right - eous will, Re - mem - ber - ing in faith - ful
save and free; Break forth with shouts of ho - ly
with the lyre, With voic - es praise the sov - 'reign
of all lands, Let moun - tains join and shout for
mel - o - dy! For God will judge with right - eous -

things, Whose hand brings vic - to - ry!
love The house of Is - ra - el.
joy; All lands, make mel - o - dy.
God, O rous - ing, joy - ous choir.
joy, Let riv - ers clap their hands.
ness And rule with eq - ui - ty.

# 460

## SIYAHAMBA

Traditional African melody
Additional music by **DÉSIRÉE GOYETTE**
Arranged by **ED BOGAS**

Zulu text
Additional text by
**DÉSIRÉE GOYETTE**

* Optional original Zulu text
(written: Si-ya-hamb' e-ku-kha-nyen' kwen-khos, pronounced: See-yah-hahm-buh koo-kah-nyen-ne kwen-kohs)

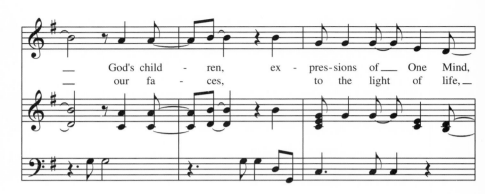

God's child - ren, ex - pres-sions of __ One Mind,
our fa - ces, to the light of life, __

__ liv - ing in__ the ra - diance of
__ har - mon - y__ re - pla - ces__

Spir - it all__ di - vine.__ Ev-'ry heart__ and na -
pain and fear and strife. __ See the heav-__ 'nly har -

_____ tion _____ is an - swer - ing _____ the call
_____ vest _____ boun - ti - ful - ly poured,

_____ to a true _____ sal - va - tion _____ know - ing
_____ as we raise _____ our voi - ces _____

*2nd time D.S. al Coda*   *Coda*

God is All _____ in all. _____   2. We are _____
all in one _____ ac - cord! _____   3. We are

# 461

**CHAPEL HILL** 884.484.
**KEVIN McCARTER**

**ALL-PRESENCE**
**PETER J. HENNIKER-HEATON**

♩ = 76-84

1. We can-not turn a - way from God be - cause, which - ev - er
2. Wheth - er we turn to left or right, to north or south or
3. Wheth - er we plunge to o - cean trench or plot our course for
4. Wheth - er we build for cen - turies hence or let to - mor - row

way we face, Spir - it is there. In ev - ery place,
east or west, we meet with Love— and we are blessed.
far - thest space, Love's law con - trols. What - ev - er race we
bound our aim, God sets the pace. Al - ways the same, with

ev - ery di - rec - tion, ev - ery - where, Spir - it is there.
Up - ward or down, be - low, a - bove, we meet with Love.
en - ter toward what - ev - er goals, Love's law con - trols.
in - stant and e - ter - nal grace, God sets the pace.

# 462

**SANCHEZ**
**SUSAN MACK**
Arranged by **SUE LOOMIS**
and **ROBERT ROCKABRAND**

SIMPLY PRAISING HIM
**SUSAN MACK**

1. When my heart is lost in sor - row, and light seems far and
2. (When) wea - ri - ness en - gulfs me, dis - cour - age - ment sinks
3. (When my) days are much too bus - y to find where prayer fits

dim, There's a ten - der prayer I can al - ways pray:
in, There's a hope - ful prayer I can al - ways pray:
in, There's a time - less prayer I can al - ways pray:

*Refrain*

Sim - ply prais - ing Him. Praise the Cre - a - tor. Let
Sim - ply prais - ing Him. Praise the Cre - a - tor. Let
Sim - ply prais - ing Him. Praise the Cre - a - tor. Let

*Refrain*

Praise the Cre - a - tor. Let all with - in me sing! For

that's what I am made to do, and good - ness it will bring. For

that's what we are made to do, let all the earth now sing!

# INDEXES

# TUNES, ALPHABETICAL

*Where the meter is irregular or unspecified, none is shown.*

# TUNES, METRICAL

# Composers and Sources

# Authors and Sources

# FIRST LINES

*First lines of hymns by Mary Baker Eddy are printed in italics.*
*Other settings found in the* Christian Science Hymnal *are also indicated.*